MOVING ON

Also by Stuart Perrin

Dancing Man: A Deeper Sense of Surrender
Leah: A Story of Meditation and Healing
The Mystical Ferryboat
A Deeper Surrender: Notes on a Spiritual Life

MOVING ON

Finding Happiness in a Changed World

STUART PERRIN

HAMPTON ROADS
PUBLISHING COMPANY, INC.
for the evolving human spirit

Cover design by Jane Hagaman
Cover art © Creatas/Brand X Pictures. All rights reserved.

Hampton Roads Publishing Company, Inc.
1125 Stoney Ridge Road
Charlottesville, VA 22902
434-296-2772
fax: 434-296-5096
800-766-8009 (orders only)
e-mail: hrpc@hrpub.com
www.hrpub.com

Library of Congress Cataloging-in-Publication Data

Perrin, Stuart, 1942-
  Moving on : finding happiness in a changed world / Stuart Perrin.
    p. cm.
  ISBN 1-57174-371-5 (5-1/2x6-1/2 tp : alk. paper)
  1. Spiritual life--Quotations, maxims, etc. I. Title.
  BL624.P4545 2004
  204'.32--dc22

                                    2004000744

                   ISBN 1-57174-371-5

                   10 9 8 7 6 5 4 3 2 1

           Printed on acid-free paper in Canada

To my wonderful daughter,
Ania Devi, at eight years old.

Introduction

In those quiet moments, when the noise of the day and the noise of our minds and emotions abate and leave us time to delve into meaningful and deeper reminders of why we are alive, the rough and tumble of daily living subsides and we are in touch with a wellspring of deep inner silence.

The insights of this book will guide the reader past confusion of conflicting thoughts and dreamlike images he or she thinks are real, into a reality devoid of illusion, a reality that cuts through a painful and dense fog blinding people to their true selves. The question will be asked: "Who am I?" And the answer will surprise the reader. It will show a multifaceted person capable of transforming suffering into joy and happiness. It will allow the reader to move on and to find happiness no matter how much the world has changed. It will help the lotus flower to emerge from muddy waters.

Rudi

Rudi was an American-born spiritual teacher and meditation master who lived in New York City. He trained many disciples in a spiritual practice that gave them the strength to transform the tensions and confusions of daily living into an open heart and a connection with Higher Creative Energy in the Universe. He died in an airplane crash in 1973. He spent many years of his life learning from great masters in India and adapted ancient Hindu and Buddhist teachings to Western living. He embraced life and all its difficulties and found God hiding behind the thousands of masks we see in front of us every day.

*W*hen a human being uses will

to dictate the ways of the world,

he spends his time manipulating shadows.

$\mathcal{W}$e trip and stumble over life's obstacles

till life's obstacles remind us that only spirit is infinite.

Everything else is finite and limited,

a piece of a puzzle,

mere steps on a ladder leading to God.

We refuse to live in the moment,

but drift with mind and emotion

from the past to the future,

unaware of a simple reality:

This moment contains what is, was, and will be.

If we continue to drift unconsciously

from moment to moment,

life's splendor slips right past us.

To love without consciousness
is to wander blindly in another person's heart.

$\mathcal{W}$e regard suffering with disdain,
but without it, we lose one of life's best teachers.

*I*t is better to be wrong and grow

by making up the difference,

than to be right and crystallized

in our own point of view.

To try to understand the logic of the world
is like placing a gallon of water in a six-ounce glass.

*H*ow many people can remember

the color of the socks they wore yesterday?

How many people can remember

what they had for breakfast

or the reason why they argued with a loved one?

*L*iving in the past is like
drawing a wagon with a dead ox.

$\mathcal{M}$editation brings together

life's discordant elements.

It creates harmony and balance within a human being;

it dredges up inner garbage, flushes it out,

and gives us a taste of transcendental energy.

Hunger for spiritual food is the first step

on a path to enlightenment.

*W*e're up against ourselves.

We are the problem

and we're also the solution to the problem.

The Earth is often compared to a circus,

but the truth is,

no one goes to the circus to have a lousy time.

To find one happy person on Earth
is more difficult than finding the Holy Grail.

A wise man knows nothing,

but a fool is convinced

his knowledge will change the world.

A wise man admits his limitations.

He lets life be and he loves people

for who and what they are.

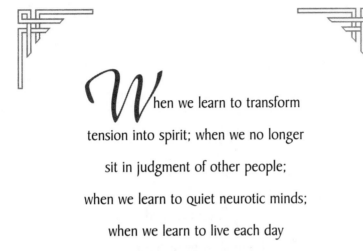

When we learn to transform
tension into spirit; when we no longer
sit in judgment of other people;
when we learn to quiet neurotic minds;
when we learn to live each day
with harmony and balance;
when we're grateful for the things that bother us;
when we learn the above;
and, more importantly, when we live it,
we are well on our warrior's path to enlightenment.

*L*ike the wind,

I drift in many directions

before I find my path out of the world.

*I*nnocence without foundation
is like veneered furniture in a rainstorm.

There is change
in that which appears stagnant:
water evaporates, the body grows old.

A stagnant pool of water

attracts insects and disease.

Anyone can drink from a stream

that flows down a mountain.

To define freedom? Impossible.

The words themselves are a prison.

Freedom is not what we possess,

but how detached we are from our possessions.

*U*ntil the world learns to forgive

terror, war, vengeance, and hate, all the vehicles

of death and destruction will plague mankind.

But forgiveness starts with each of us.

First we must forgive ourselves.

We have nothing to be guilty of,

nothing to be fearful of, nothing but our inability

to center ourselves and keep our hearts open.

We all want to live wonderful lives,

but wonderment of life cannot exist

if we tear ourselves apart, if we look into a mirror

and do not see what's there.

$\mathcal{L}$ ife is the mirror.

It reflects every human being's view of reality.

It shows us how important it is to forgive.

The moment we open our hearts and love,

the moment we learn to be happy,

forgiveness finds its way to the core of our being.

We let the world be.

We see suffering in every person's eyes

and realize suffering

brings us all closer to the universal spirit.

$\mathcal{F}$orgiveness is a teaching

that has been passed down through the ages,

yet it's never listened to nor recognized

for its importance in humankind's survival.

Forgiveness opens the heart

and lets us live in the radiance of love.

*P*eople suffer from self-inflicted terrorism

when fear paralyzes true creativity.

But the closer they get to embracing spirit,

the less there is to fear.

Life and death disappear in a oneness of vision

touching on the divine.

The first step

in the direction of world harmony will be taken

when people stop terrorizing themselves.

Terrorism has been around a long time.

I don't mean fundamentalist terrorism,

but the terror people experience in their daily lives.

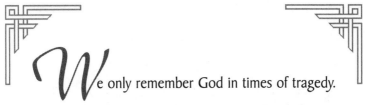

We only remember God in times of tragedy.

At all other times, most people are too busy

to remember God or humanity

or goodness and spiritual work.

They assume the bubble will never burst.

When it finally bursts, millions of people

rush to holy places to ask for God's help.

They don't realize the most sacred place on Earth

is the spot they are standing.

If they muck up that spot, they disconnect themselves

from the soul of the universe.

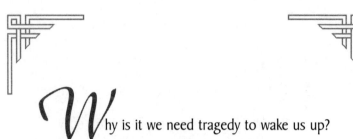

Why is it we need tragedy to wake us up?

Why does tragedy remind us

there's goodness in the human heart?

Will people remember after September 11

that love and joy are what makes us human?

I think we've all been given a wake up call—an

opportunity to rekindle the heart,

to forgive one another

and embrace the universal spirit.

*H*appy people don't fight wars.

They live with compassion and forgiveness.

But it's rare to find a happy person.

Thus we have war and terrorism

and we will continue to have them

until every human being finds inner peace.

It's a long process, but the results are worth it.

Nobody wants to fight when the heart is full of love.

*P*roblems are part of a universal design.

No matter how much we complain about them,

they never go away.

But, without them, we wouldn't work on ourselves.

The world's a mirror

reflecting the positive and negative

in every human being.

But it's absurd to think we can change ourselves

by adjusting the reflection.

If there's a pimple on our face,

we don't get rid of the pimple

by rubbing salve on the mirror.

*I*t is easy to teach what we don't know.

*B*eneath the noise of the human mind

and the tug of human emotions

is a vast wellspring of silence

so deep and pure it can be heard

in city traffic, on subways,

in restaurants, and on crowded streets.

All we have to do is listen.

*I*f I cannot forgive my family and friends,

how can they forgive me?

$\mathcal{N}$ature has mastered death and rebirth

and cycles of change.

It surrenders to life and death without effort . . .

a natural and organic process

foreign to most human beings.

If we sit at the master's feet,

we learn how gracefully winter becomes spring.

ost human beings live

in the shadow of their enlightened selves.

They refuse to step out of the shadow

and allow the heart to determine action.

But the shadow world has its own unique qualities

that sidetrack us and give us what to do every day,

that make room for the mad and the blind

to dance a funny little dance

at the edge of a foggy cliff.

I've never known certainty in my life

nor have "things" of the world made me secure.

The only time fog lifts is when I feel inner peace.

*L*ove is the very source of creation

and we, fools that we are,

cut ourselves off from creation

and wander about the Earth

looking everywhere for answers

that are in the center of our hearts.

*T*here's nothing more wonderful

than spiritual growth.

It's an adventure

that pits each of us against ourselves.

But the path through the inner world

is unique to every voyager

and the path to the other side of us

is the path to God.

The most sacred place on Earth

is the spot you are standing.

Once you realize this, all seeking is over.

*B*eneath noise there's a silence so profound

it consumes the universe.

The silence is deep inside us.

It waits patiently for us to uncover its secrets.

It's our work to find silence,

not the work of silence to find us.

*P*eople think meditation practice

is for wimps, flakes, and weirdos,

but real meditation weeds them all out.

$\mathcal{F}$ind a married couple

practicing deep spiritual work every day

and you'll probably find a healthy relationship.

*I*t takes great strength and inner security

to respect the uniqueness of another individual's life.

Why suffocate them with ego?

Why snuff out their creative energy?

Why lecture them on the right way to live?

The end goal of desire is happiness,

but rarely, if ever, do rewards make us happy.

We, alone, can make ourselves happy.

All we have to do is open our hearts.

The only successful person on Earth

is a happy person.

*W*hen the heart opens

a twinkle of light appears in the eyes . . .

a beauty no fashion magazine can capture,

no makeup artist or hair stylist can create,

a beauty radiating from the human soul.

*S*eeking happiness in the outer world
is like trying to imprison a gallery of shadows.

*I*nsecure people put others down;

sick minds and hearts revel in

misfortune, failure, and human misery.

*I*t takes years of meditation practice

to develop security;

to conquer jealousy, pettiness,

smallness of mind, and opinion,

and not for a moment believe our lives

are more important than other people's.

"*I*t takes nine months to have a baby

and one second to die."

Rudi

The moment we strive

for money, success, relationships, etc.,

at that very moment we attract to ourselves

all the difficulty of the undertaking.

If there were no difficulty,

we'd never learn to transform problems into success.

We would live like cabbage heads in a small garden

quietly waiting to be picked.

In every generation there are a handful of people who have an idea of what's going on. Everyone else is busy being important.

The only person I live with
twenty-four hours a day is myself.

If I don't make friends with me,

how am I going to make friends with other people?

*P*roblems don't go away.

They will be with us as long as we are alive.

But if we master our inner selves,

problems are no longer problems,

they are opportunities to grow

and have an extraordinary life.

*I*t's the right of every human being

to live a wonderful life.

We're not born to be miserable and unhappy.

An infant radiates joy and sweetness . . .

everything precious the world has to offer.

Where does it disappear?

Why do we have to spend the rest of our lives

regaining what we're born with?

o one on Earth
will act or react as we think they should.

We have to accept people as they are.

I've never had a positive experience

that wasn't followed by its opposite.

It's the same with negative experiences.

They are both a reflection

of an active mind projecting its own reality.

Neither leads to spiritual enlightenment.

We must learn to unify positive and negative;

we must learn to transform them

into harmony and balance.

*I*t's foolish to think that because one meditates

one is having a spiritual life.

The real test of a spiritual life

is what happens to us when we leave the temple.

*I*f we don't build a bridge

between meditation class and the rest of life,

we clutter ourselves with wisdom

that has no practical use.

*O*nce we trust life,

we're no longer afraid to live it.

Every person, every situation becomes our teacher.

We must bow to our teacher.

We must learn from him.

We must see that God exists

in every nook and cranny of the universe.

$\mathcal{M}$editation class is like a gym.

We go there to work out,

to build chakras and a strong inner life,

but meditation class becomes our limitation

if we believe

it's the beginning and end of God's terrain.

There is no activity on Earth
that somehow doesn't fit into God's design:
A policeman needs criminals or he has no job;
a garbage man needs garbage
and a firefighter needs fires.
We all need problems
or we'd never do anything about ourselves.

 *T*he outer world,

with its kaleidoscopic confusion,

reflects the inner world of every human being.

If we want to clear up the confusion,

we have to go to its source,

we have to dredge muddy internal waters,

sift through them and dissolve encumbrances

that keep our creativity from flowing.

The freer we are of ourselves,

the freer we are of the outer world.

*E*very human being

lives at the center of creation.

All he or she has to do is see it.

*W*hen our hearts are full of joy,

love, and gratitude, the spirit of God

can be seen in a twinkle of light

radiating from our eyes.

*L*ife is hard, but so what!

We all need roughage.

If we don't have roughage in our diet,

our digestive systems get messed up.

We'd never go to the toilet.

Life's difficulty is part of a healthy diet.

It can be used to grow.

It can be transformed into positive energy.

You just have to know how to do it.

You have to get proper training.

No one can hurt us unless we let them,

not if we open our hearts, feel love, joy, forgiveness,

and the rest of the higher emotions.

It is a different kind of logic,

one that trusts the world and that trusts one's self.

It takes a very strong person to live with trust.

I can never remember it being any different,

not in my childhood, teenage years,

twenties, or thirties.

There was always the battle of opposites

consuming every moment of my time.

Always, goodness followed by evil.

So, when good things happen, I stay detached;

when negative things happen,

I still remained detached.

I've seen "The Good" put on demon masks

and spit fire in my face;

I've used negative experiences as steps on a ladder

leading to profound spiritual growth.

There are billions of people on Earth.

Every one of them sees a different reality.

Somewhere along the way

there needs to be compromise.

one of us is perfect.

We'll all have problems until the day we die.

Since perfection is the domain

of God and His angels and madmen,

inner growth is the best we mortals can do.

We evolve closer to perfection.

Our problems are reminders that we're not perfect;

we have to work on ourselves;

we can't take ourselves for granted.

A job is a place to learn about ourselves,

to become more conscious of who or what we are,

to refine our abilities

and use them the best we can on Earth.

*A*mbition releases torrents of tension

that sweep us away

in emotional and psychological tides,

often washing us out to sea.

It can also guide us to spirit.

It all depends on how we use it, or how it uses us.

No one succeeds in life

without experiencing failure.

One attracts the other. People afraid to fail live

in little worlds of self-inflicted perfection,

frightened worlds bordering the unknown.

They never take a chance.

Ambition attracts success and failure.

It forces us to sally forth in life's adventure;

to slay dragons, griffins, and motley monsters;

to find the pot of gold or damsel in distress.

In truth, there is no such thing as failure.

There are only mistakes.

We need to learn from them and go on.

*T*here's no guarantee

we're going to succeed in life.

We have to take each day at a time

and measure our self-worth

by the amount of openness in our hearts,

by our mastery of tension,

and by our ability to live quietly in the moment.

$\mathcal{W}$e can't compare ourselves with other people.

There is no sense in it.

No matter how successful we become,

there's always someone more successful.

*S*atisfaction limits life to old,

boring, and repetitive activities.

The only thing that grows is one's ass.

*W*e're born on Earth to learn to serve.

Wittingly or unwittingly,

we serve some part of life,

but unconditional service teaches unconditional love.

It expects nothing in return

for time spent helping other people,

and it lifts the consciousness of a human being

bogged down in self-interest.

*I*f "God is love"

and the spectacle of God is all around us,

then everything is steeped in love.

Our work is to bow to God's love

in the hearts of men. It is to forgive and have

patience and not judge the mistakes of others,

to be free of ourselves and be one with God,

to be a vehicle for spiritual energy, and never,

not for a moment, think we are doing it.

It is to trust the world and its lessons, to surrender

opinion and ego, and to be grateful for every morsel

of food and every experience (both positive

and negative) and recognize it as our teacher.

The prime purpose of money is to give life.

It is not a goal unto itself.

*W*e alone can make ourselves happy.

Once we learn this, we can share joy and happiness

with other human beings.

We stop searching for the elusive butterfly.

We've discovered happiness exists within ourselves.

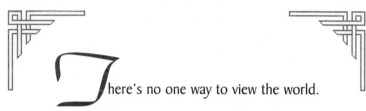

There's no one way to view the world.

What's right and wrong, what's positive and negative,

are simply states of mind.

But the heart doesn't judge.

The heart teaches us to be human.

The compassion of Schindler (of *Schindler's List*)

arose from looking evil directly in the eye

and not being afraid.

Without Nazi fanaticism staring him in the face,

his nobility of soul may never have surfaced.

Fascist horrors turned him into a saintly person.

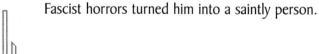

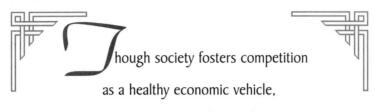

Though society fosters competition

as a healthy economic vehicle,

the pressures of competition

deteriorate mental and physical well-being.

The body breaks down. The mind lapses into

black holes of forgetfulness. There's jealousy,

backbiting, ass kicking, and hundreds

of other reactions to competitive society.

People are nervous wrecks.

They can't handle the pressure. But in truth, no one

is in competition with anyone else.

There's abundance enough to provide for every living

person. If we get past ourselves, the rest is easy.

*W*e can succeed in life

without shredding our minds and bodies.

The first step is internal, to build a strong inner life.

The object is to get balanced, open the heart,

quiet the mind, listen to the voice of silence emerging

from transcendental planes of consciousness,

and create a bridge connecting meditation practice

to every other area of life.

eople want to be pampered

and cuddled and told the pain will pass,

but pain lingers until the day we die.

We have to make friends with it;

we have to detach ourselves

from its gnawing presence.

Rich and poor both inhabit

six-foot parcels of land

in which flesh and bones are food for worms,

yet the mind refuses to dwell on nothingness.

It refuses to see past death's blind spot,

to recognize the illusive

and temporary nature of the dream we call life.

We all have to learn to joyfully embrace death.

We have no choice in the matter.

*W*e're born, we live, and we die.

There's no escaping that reality.

We have to embrace all three.

They remind us no one is walking around on Earth

from the seventeenth century.

inety-eight percent

of the world's tension

comes from money and relationships.

*S*ilence is our best friend.
It is the voice of God

made manifest inside every human being.

When we meditate on silence,

it grows to encompass thought, sound, music,

city noise; all of the above become remote gurgles

in a great wellspring.

We become the silence.

$\mathcal{U}$nconditional giving

is the heart's extension of love and gratitude

made manifest in the world.

The giver has no preconceived expectations.

He gives because it is a joy to give.

He serves because service is a path to God.

It is one-half of a necessary cycle

completing his humanity.

The other half is unconditional receiving.

*W*hen we combine joy with responsibility,

our cycles of karma come to a screeching halt.

They shift and change as we change inside ourselves.

They are not a stagnant force.

To accept the present
is to free ourselves from karma.
To fight it is to create more karma,
more reasons to reincarnate,
and more difficulty and tension.

$\mathcal{T}$alk of reincarnation turns to nonsense

the moment we realize

there's only one life lived throughout eternity.

The moment we desire someone
or something on Earth, be it success,
marriage, objects, money, or a spiritual life,
we have to prepare ourselves
for the repercussions of desire.
As long as we desire worldly possessions,
there will be pain.
Even the desire for enlightenment attracts pain.

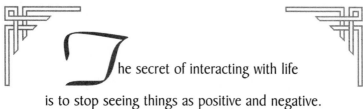

The secret of interacting with life

is to stop seeing things as positive and negative.

Each situation is another reason

to go deeper within our self.

It is not a reason to bitch and complain

and fight with other human beings.

They are not the enemy.

They are mostly unconscious people

struggling with their own lives.

They should remind us to stay centered,

to go deeper, to not let petty differences and tensions

rip away the benefits of meditation.

*S*uccess at life

depends on how happy we are

at the moment of death.

Success at life

also depends on a conscious dialectic:

Are life and death one and the same to us?

Can we embrace them?

Are we no longer frightened of the unknown?

*I*f we have found the spiritual child in us,

if our inner lives are vital, happy, full of joy and love,

though the body will have its share

of aches and pains,

age will do little or nothing

to stop the evolution of higher consciousness.

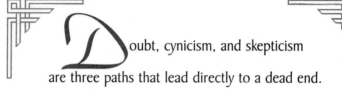

*D*oubt, cynicism, and skepticism

are three paths that lead directly to a dead end.

They are created from threads of fear

that keep people

from ever stepping into the unknown.

They stop the creative process by reducing insight,

imagination, instinct, and improvisation

to structured mindsets that have answers

before questions are even asked.

Doubt and skepticism

siphon creative juice from people.

They leave us empty, dead, and sterile, and they

destroy the possibility of living life in the moment.

*A*pathy and detachment

are very different issues.

Apathetic people care little or nothing about life.

They are usually lazy, unproductive,

irresponsible souls avoiding pressure

and commitment as if both were diseases.

Detachment is another thing.

We can't detach ourselves

from what we haven't experienced.

To be truly detached,

we have to be at the center of life.

We have to be active, creative people

unafraid to explore whatever avenue life opens to us.

ew York City reminds me

to stay centered,

to stay balanced, and to work on myself every day.

I like its bumps and grinds.

I like the pressures and distractions.

They force me to discipline myself.

The symbol for Buddhism

is the lotus flower.

Lotus flowers grow out of mud.

Human beings also grow out of mud.

They, too, have to learn to float on muddy water.

$\mathcal{M}$editation practice teaches us
to return to basics.

We need to be well rooted on Earth.

*T*he greatest teachers

speak about forgiveness—

a trait important to learn for no other reason

than it relieves us of resentment and anger.

It allows us to move on.

*W*e must develop awareness
of the dependency we have on all living creatures.

The child in us trusts life,

God, goodness in the world,

simplicity, and potential for spiritual growth.

It is attacked every day by armies of cynicism.

But, by hook or crook,

it survives an unbelieving world

and continues to search for God.

When people discover their inner child,

usually after years of deep spiritual work

and conviction, the inner child changes them.

They enter its Edenlike nursery. There, they nurture

themselves on love, goodness, innocence, and trust.

There, they learn to speak God's language on Earth.

The dramas of life are like a fart in a hurricane.

*I*t doesn't take vast wealth

and power to be happy.

All it takes is an open heart.

*I*t takes great strength
to live in the moment, to resurrect ourselves
from pasts full of guilt, fear, and unhappiness,
and enjoy whatever we do. It takes great strength
to have three hundred and sixty-four
"un-birthday" parties, to not get stuck
in emotional and psychological mud.
It's easy to complain about injustice
and life's peccadilloes, but life isn't going to change.
We have to change. We have to remind ourselves
that every day is New Year's.
The present doesn't go away. It's always with us.
Everything else disappears in the past.

*W*e live with expectations

and we defeat ourselves when the ends

are not what we imagined they'd be.

What if we expected nothing?

If we accepted our gifts as they came?

If an empty sky was at the end of every struggle?

Imagine the joy we would take

in the things we found along the way.

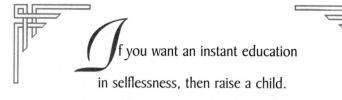

*I*f you want an instant education

in selflessness, then raise a child.

She cries at three or four o'clock in the morning

without regard to time or place. She's either hungry

or has wet her bed or is scared. And it doesn't mat-

ter how tired you are. You still have to find that extra

bit of energy. There's no use complaining.

She won't listen. Her only way of reaching you is by

crying, and it is never without a reason. Sometimes

she wants to be held or fed. Sometimes to be spoken

to or sung to. If you love someone,

it transforms you into a minor league martyr.

There isn't much time for yourself.

*E*verything is a mystery in a child's world.
She can create a magic kingdom from wooden sticks
or paper matches or sipping straws. She talks to
imaginary friends, make-believe pets, and nature
spirits. Give her a crayon and she'll produce
a masterpiece. It's all a mystery and has newness.
She has no categories for her experience, but loves
without condition and is always reaching into the
unknown. Just think if the day to day activities adults
take for granted became a mystery. If they experienced for the first time eating with a fork,
flushing the toilet, getting into bed,
clothing themselves. We would never be bored.

*W*hatever we understand

becomes our limitation

if we accept it as ultimate truth.

One learns by way of paradox,

by defying the mind,

by seeing that spiritual energy has logic of its own.

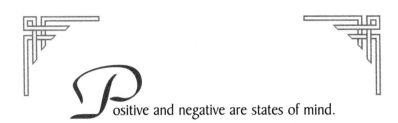

ositive and negative are states of mind.

If we accept one as the truth,

the other will come along moments later

and kick us in the ass.

It does not matter if we are right or wrong,

only that we are growing.

As long as we cling to one notion of the world,

we are dead men.

We are trapped in a circle of familiar things

and can find no way out.

The seeker after truth is a warrior.

His battlefield is strewn with the remains of self-image

and he continues to destroy self-image until he dies

or frees himself from it

and continues on the path to enlightenment.

*C*reative energy is so vast

and of such an intense nature

that it is impossible to consume it whole.

We must nibble at it first.

As we get stronger,

we can eat greater quantities of food.

$\mathcal{W}$e live in a world
that values instant gratification.
No one values patience and discipline
or understands the amount of work it takes
to become a master of oneself.

*I*magine if everyone knew the date of his death;

imagine if they knew exactly how much time

they would have before they left this world.

Each moment would be precious.

Even trivial things would take on a golden sheen.

*I*t takes years of study

to become a master chef, a neurosurgeon,

an artist, musician, writer,

furniture maker, electrician, or plumber.

The most difficult task of all

is to master one's inner life.

Why do people think they don't need teachers

to help them along the way?

$\mathcal{W}$hen I ask myself:

What's easy? I think: TV dinners are easy.

McDonalds, Burger King,

and Kentucky Fried Chicken are easy.

A gourmet meal takes hours to prepare.

Junk food takes seconds to mess up our stomachs.

It takes years of training to become a master chef.

It takes a lifetime to master the confusion inside us.

*W*hat's the worst that can happen to me?

I die? All right, then my problems will disappear

and I'll have nothing to worry about anymore.

What's worse than death

is an empty shell of a person

pretending their petty dramas and soap operas

are a reason to be alive!

*S*ons are not
what parents think they should be;

sons struggle for their own identity.

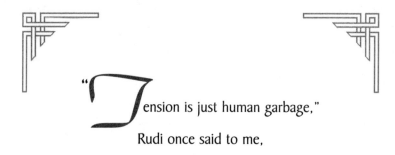

"Tension is just human garbage,"

Rudi once said to me,

"and garbage makes the best compost.

If you bring your tension to the base of the spine

and transform it into energy,

the thing that's killing you will give you life.

It's a process, a way of using all our crap,

of making room within ourselves for God.

Like the alchemist,

we transform everything into gold."

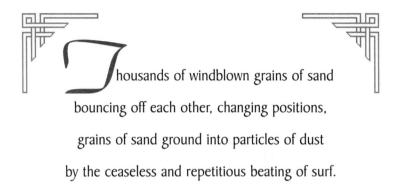

Thousands of windblown grains of sand

bouncing off each other, changing positions,

grains of sand ground into particles of dust

by the ceaseless and repetitious beating of surf.

The ocean eats continents,

streams devour mountains, mountains erupt—

time alone understands beginnings and endings.

The rest of life shifts and changes

with a seething and restless zeal.

The Earth is a minor league insane asylum

peopled with important and not-so-important people

struggling to get through the day.

*L*ike kids in bumper cars at a carnival,

ideas and opinions bounce off each other

without ever touching deeper ground.

There's so much talk and so little listening,

a lot of movement and nothing getting done.

If only we could learn to listen to each other.

If we could just surrender our self-importance.

$\mathcal{N}$othing makes us work harder

on ourselves than the "inner mess."

It reminds us that we're alive,

that we have work to do,

that we haven't arrived yet.

Trust the light side and the dark side

and everything in between.

It all has one purpose:

to get you to a deeper place in yourself.

It's foolish to think there's a gilded path to God.

Every step of the way reminds us

we have a long voyage ahead of us.

*I*t's easy to be happy

after winning a 27-million-dollar lotto jackpot.

Real nobility of soul is keeping an open heart

when taking out the garbage.

There's so much joy, love, and kindness

in the human heart.

Even when life is impossible,

joy and love need not disappear.

"*I* am not here to give you answers.

I am here to give you the energy

so that you can find your own answers

and find within you that which you are."

Rudi

A spiritual warrior sees life and death as one.

There's no duality on the battlefield,

no fear, no longing, no thoughts of victory,

nor rewards or goals.

He bows to his enemy

and finds a final resting place in love

radiating from the center of his own heart.

*W*hen we awaken the spirit inside us,

when we live our lives in the moment,

when we're no longer filled

with fragmented images of self,

we discover everything that was, is,

and will be "is" in the moment.

We don't have to look for answers

in the annals of time and history.

To search the past for answers

is like trying to steal a car

in an automobile graveyard.

*B*eneath the noise of the streets,

the voices of people, the chit-chat of the mind,

the subtle sounds of music, nature,

and every human heart beat,

there is silence so profound it consumes the universe.

*I*f we connect with silence,

we'll never lack for life's boundless spiritual treasures.

All thought, emotion, and other noise

cover up deep hunger in human beings

for silence's sublime state of grace

touching on the wisdom of God.

There was always room on my guru's table

for bagels, lox, cream cheese, roast beef,

pecan pie, astral traveling, Bardo work, business,

and total surrender to higher energy in the universe.

*P*eople are too busy living

their own soap operas without realizing

that today's soap opera becomes a piece of driftwood

floating in memory.

*P*eople live with "Why me?" complexes.

They complain about everything

and terrorize themselves,

family, friends, and neighbors.

They never look at the pain in another person's eyes,

they never see that suffering is a perfect democracy.

I spent ten years looking for a teacher capable of living what he taught. Most teachers I'd met preached the time-worn mantra "love, peace, and eat vegetables," then retreated to boring, mundane, and mediocre existences. Rudi could take a bite out of life. He lived in the moment.

He spontaneously channeled higher energy into joyous, intense, conscious, God-serving, and egoless living. His material success in no way interfered with his spiritual practice.

He saw no separation between the two. One nurtured the other. At the same time, neither controlled him.

$\mathcal{A}$fter thirty years of practicing meditation,

I've come to realize I know nothing about life.

Isn't that wonderful?

There's so much to learn and so many places to go.

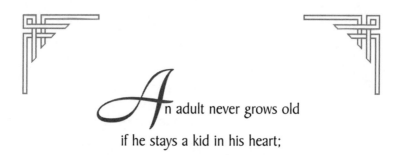

*A*n adult never grows old

if he stays a kid in his heart;

a kid never turns his back on life's possibilities;

a kid is a prophet of love in a time of hate

and anger and joy and bliss.

He joins hands with other children

and they dance in a circle of innocence.

No more promises. No more platitudes and sitcoms

and mundane preachers of gospel.

Just the circle, the dance, the genesis of all things.

The first time I tasted spiritual nectar

flowing from the crown of my head into my heart,

I realized there was nothing wrong with the world.

"People experience the astral plane

and make a big deal about it,

but the astral plane is no more

than two fingers above our heads.

Hanging out there is like slumming in the cosmos.

I'd rather be a speck of light

dissolving into the eternal;

I'd rather be nothing but love and joy

at the center of God's heart."

Rudi

"It strikes me, after a while,

even heaven itself can become a bore.

How long can we sit around

praising the Pearly Gates?

I don't think I'd want to

decorate my apartment in pastels.

Heaven's interior design would drive me crazy."

Rudi

"*S*piritual energy transcends logic,
understanding and rational thinking.

It can only be experienced through surrender."

Rudi

A spiritual life doesn't negate success,

marriage, family, friendships,

money, power, and fame.

It puts them in their true perspective.

They are steps on a ladder

that extends into the cosmos,

a ladder that connects every human being with God.

They are not ends in themselves,

but means to learn about oneself and one's karma.

*S*uffering forces people

to reevaluate their lives,

to search for new answers to timeless questions,

to touch a part of themselves in need of spirituality.

Hunger for that kind of food initiates an inner search.

It's the first step in a lifelong voyage

to the realms of the divine.

"*I*'d rather be wrong all the time.

At least I can learn something,

at least I'm not judging everyone and everything

according to my own preconceptions,

and at least there's room for humility and growth."

Rudi

*B*reath is like prayer.

Every time we inhale, we receive life, and

every time we exhale, we surrender a part of ourselves.

The mind's power opens the foundation of our being.

It brings harmony and balance

and it helps us develop strong inner lives.

It transforms tension into a life-giving force.

The question remains: How to do this?

The answer is simple: It takes training.

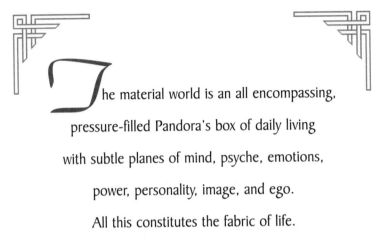

The material world is an all encompassing,

pressure-filled Pandora's box of daily living

with subtle planes of mind, psyche, emotions,

power, personality, image, and ego.

All this constitutes the fabric of life.

There's no escaping it.

It's a constant reminder we're born on Earth

and not in seraphic realms or heavenly landscapes.

We have karma to work out with parents, spouses,

children, friends, relatives,

and numerous other people we meet daily.

*E*ach day is a spectacle of creation,

a precious God-given gift to treasure

from the moment we wake up in the morning

to the moment we go to sleep at night.

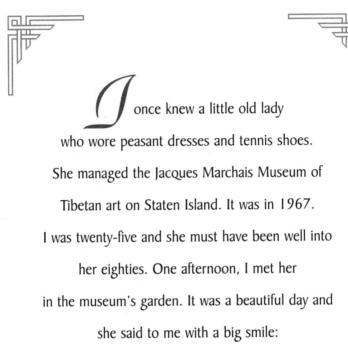

I once knew a little old lady
who wore peasant dresses and tennis shoes.
She managed the Jacques Marchais Museum of
Tibetan art on Staten Island. It was in 1967.
I was twenty-five and she must have been well into
her eighties. One afternoon, I met her
in the museum's garden. It was a beautiful day and
she said to me with a big smile:
"People are afraid of reincarnation. Me! I don't care.
I just want to come back like a spring day."

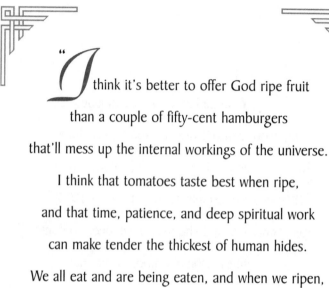

"I think it's better to offer God ripe fruit

than a couple of fifty-cent hamburgers

that'll mess up the internal workings of the universe.

I think that tomatoes taste best when ripe,

and that time, patience, and deep spiritual work

can make tender the thickest of human hides.

We all eat and are being eaten, and when we ripen,

when we're succulently overflowing with love,

it'll be a joy for God

to pluck us from our karmic vine."

Rudi

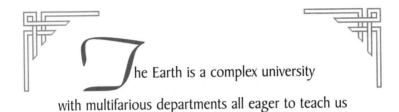

The Earth is a complex university

with multifarious departments all eager to teach us

how to get to God.

The problem is that we don't listen.

We know better than the Earth.

We argue with a great master,

an argument impossible to win,

but an argument that engages most of our time

and energy, an argument that finally exhausts us.

The energy needed to develop a spiritual life

is wasted on pettiness, vanity, greed,

avarice, and empty desire.

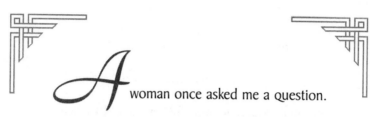

$\mathcal{A}$ woman once asked me a question.

She'd been a student for a few months.

She looked very troubled.

"How can I study with you?" she asked.

"I'm a lesbian."

"I don't care if you sleep with sheep," I said to her.

"Do you want to grow closer to God?"

"Yes," she said.

"Then you qualify to have a spiritual life. I cannot

judge a person. I can only love them and help them

to work out their life."

$\mathcal{M}$editation practitioners

become conscious of the fact

that the inner life of a human being never grows old.

The more developed the chakra system,

the more opportunity there is

to reverse the physical and mental aging process.

As our creative capacity grows with age,

so does our wisdom

and understanding of life and death.

"Sexual energy is the Tantric vehicle

bridging the Earth and the cosmos,

the prime mover in life as we know it

and life seen in deep meditation trances.

It gives birth to the world and it gives birth

inside each and every one of us.

When used consciously,

it transforms the human into the divine."

Rudi

"*N*ext summer, at Big Indian,"

Rudi said to me a few months after

I became a teacher in his lineage,

"first I'll teach, then you'll teach,

then we'll show cartoons."

*E*veryone is already enlightened

but few people know it.

We're all just catching up to ours.

*I*t's easy to forget we have karma
and responsibility and day-to-day lives.
It's easy to become an astral vaudevillian
putting on a magic show.
Power is very attractive
and astral power is the most attractive of all,
but chakra systems have checks and balances.
Humility, love, gratitude—each of these
is a safeguard against power.
Each transforms cosmic madness into Divine light.

*H*istory has shown

that murderers can become saints,

that thieves can become holy men

and magicians can become men of God.

Change is the cornerstone of spiritual work's

ongoing process linking moment to moment.

Its force defies human logic.

The human heart says,

"I'm not better than anyone else,"

but the human mind says,

"My religion, race, gender, country, or economics

makes me superior to other people."

The mind turns a human being

into a caricature of itself.

I once taught a meditation class in a halfway house in Fort Worth, Texas, to a group of teenagers ranging from fifteen to eighteen years of age. I spoke about spiritual hunger. "If you were starving to death in a desert," I said, "and smelled a hamburger a mile away, you would find the energy to get to it."

"Yeah," one of the kids said, "but if you ate the whole hamburger at once, you'd die on the spot."

*G*od hides behind thousands of masks.

He's a master quick-change artist, a magician,

a vaudeville performer, trickster,

wise man, beggar, and fool.

He never fits any single role,

but is always present in the life dramas

that play out through time and history.

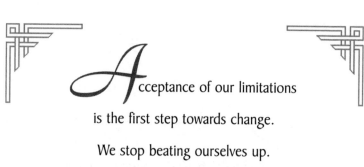

Acceptance of our limitations

is the first step towards change.

We stop beating ourselves up.

We become the best janitor, waiter, C.E.O.,

salesman, clerk, president, seamstress,

or taxi driver it's possible to be.

We should be grateful for whatever we do

for no other reason than gratitude

moves something in the heart.

It takes us to a higher place inside ourselves.

If we can't mop the floor with an open heart,

we'll never be happy running the company.

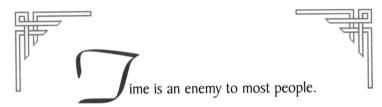

*T*ime is an enemy to most people.

They fear age and death and disease

and most of the ravages that come with growing old.

But time befriends us

when we work deeply on ourselves.

A minute becomes a day, a day a year,

and a year a minute. We don't age in an ordinary way.

Our inner life gets younger

and every moment becomes precious

when we discover we are living

at the center of creation.

*R*esponsibility to God is a terrifying thought

that would disrupt the bowels

of a character in a Dostoevsky novel.

Imagine not being able to turn your back on God.

Imagine a life full of honesty,

truthfulness, trust, and forgiveness.

A life that is beyond our comprehension.

The very thought can make people

work on themselves till the day they die.

*S*itting in the radiance of the guru's grace

without practicing deep meditation

will provide nothing but sunburn.

*G*od waits patiently

for each human soul to evolve.

Just as a pear has to ripen on a tree

before we pick it, we also have to mature and ripen.

Premature picking

makes for sour pears and bitter people.

The heart of an artichoke

is at the center of layer upon layer of bitter peels.

The closer we get to the center,

the sweeter and more delicious

the artichoke becomes.

The heart is a delicacy, a treat worth opening.

*B*reath is prayer.

Every time we inhale we take in life.

When we exhale, we surrender a part of ourselves.

We forget that every human being

is praying twenty-four hours a day.

People live with "rent control" mentality.

They struggle to find situations

that do not tax their creative abilities.

They nest in the possible.

But real creative growth and expansion

is found outside the possible.

When we make the impossible possible,

we've learned to step into the unknown

and use it for inner growth.

I've never met a pure person

and no one gets rooted

and builds a strong inner foundation

by hopping from bed to bed.

Moderation is the key to deep spiritual growth.

*S*uccess is a difficult thing to attain in life only because people are afraid to have it.

A student once asked Rudi: "Why do you

wear orange all the time?"

"Orange is the color of surrender," he answered.

"But what are you surrendering?"

"Tension," Rudi answered with a big smile.

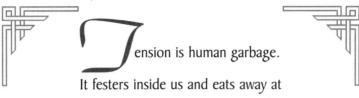

Tension is human garbage.
It festers inside us and eats away at
mind, body, and soul. There are three ways to use
tension. The first is to transform tension into *chi* by
learning to focus the mind below the navel,
by opening the third chakra, and using our tension to
build harmony and balance. The second is to use
tension to build our lives: relationships, businesses,
jobs, etc. If we channel tension into external projects,
we transform what's killing us into success
and a better life. Finally, we have to surrender the
overflow of tension not transformed into *chi*
or used to become successful in life.

There's a simple exercise

for letting go of tension:

Let your arms drop to your sides,

close your eyes and ask for help

to surrender all negative psychic tension.

The tension will flow off the ends of your fingertips.

This simple lesson can take what's killing you

and use it to give life.

$\mathcal{F}$ind a person with joy and gratitude in his heart,

a person with a quiet mind and strong foundation,

and you'll find a true human being.

The goal is not to become spiritual,

it's to become human.

Once we get the human thing down,

the spiritual finds a home inside us.

*B*uried beneath tension's rubble

is a rich, profound, incredibly beautiful,

energy-filled cauldron of truth and wisdom.

We're like watermelons,

coconuts, pecans, and pistachios.

We have to be broken open

to get to the meat or juice.

Happy people are not idiot savants,

simpletons, or lobotomized potato-heads

staring into space twenty-four hours a day.

They work, they struggle,

and they take on responsibility,

but they perform these impossible feats

with an open heart.

There are a few people who die without regret.

They learned to live simply;

they learned to expect nothing more from life

than the breath they take with them

wherever they go.

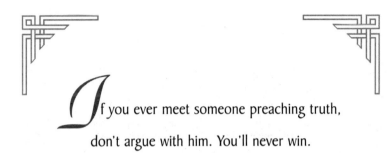

*I*f you ever meet someone preaching truth,

don't argue with him. You'll never win.

Just bow to him, walk away, and remind yourself

to live your own life

without knowing better than anyone else.

Remind yourself that definitive truth

can be very dangerous.

No single goal should become an end in itself.

Each is a step on a ladder, just another opportunity

to learn and to surrender to God.

$\mathcal{B}$oth success and failure
find their place in the design of the universe.

*T*houghts never go away.
They'll always chatter in our brains

like thousands of birds

flitting in trees on a hot summer's morning.

We just have to be strong enough

inside ourselves not to listen.

When we serve higher energy,

we take full responsibility for our lives,

karma, the planet we live on, our homes,

families, friends, and jobs.

It can't be done without deep inner strength.

Life's a good reminder that unconditional giving

and receiving are important

if we're to live here like human beings.

*K*ids are the last vestige of sanity on Earth.

They're untouched, almost pure, and color blind,

and they know how to laugh better than adults,

with a laughter that fills a room

with light and love and simple joy.

*I*f a child can't make mistakes,

he's not a child. He's an adult in a toddler's body,

a frightened adult, immobile, paralyzed,

scared to move left or right.

He's swimming in fear and doesn't know it.

*I*f a child enjoys being eleven,

maybe, just maybe, when he's thirty,

he'll enjoy being thirty.

If we kill the child in him,

we kill everything sacred in the world.

*O*pinions float across the Earth

like seeds blowing in the wind.

You never know where they're going to land

and what's going to come back.

We can pick people apart all we want.

That's not hard. If we look at them,

we're bound to find something wrong.

I've never met a perfect person.

I've met more than a few

who have assumed the role of God,

but human perfection's about as extinct as dinosaurs.

*I*t's much harder to find things

wrong with oneself than with other people.

It's hard being gracious enough to say: "I blew it.

I really screwed up. I'm wrong and I apologize."

That, at least, is a beginning

if you want to be someone's friend.

*C*onscious work

is a moment-to-moment transformation of pressure

and responsibility into spiritual energy.

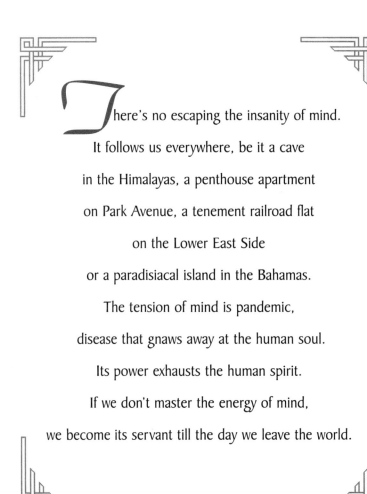

There's no escaping the insanity of mind.

It follows us everywhere, be it a cave

in the Himalayas, a penthouse apartment

on Park Avenue, a tenement railroad flat

on the Lower East Side

or a paradisiacal island in the Bahamas.

The tension of mind is pandemic,

disease that gnaws away at the human soul.

Its power exhausts the human spirit.

If we don't master the energy of mind,

we become its servant till the day we leave the world.

Today's outcasts are not thieves,
bandits, or terrorists. They're children wondering
what happened to honor and love. They're God's
little beggars waiting for truth to manifest.
They walk a lonely path between Heaven and Earth.
Today's outcasts see too much, feel too much, and
believe in goodness too much to let the world take it
away from them. They try to keep from falling into a
pit full of poisonous snakes. But I have another idea.

The outcasts could live in the pit,
keep their innocence, and fight off the snakes.

They could be newfangled heroes
sporting nobility of soul.

The child in all of us

is the blessed outcast in disguise.

With the help of God,

the child won't vanish

no matter how much pain it feels.

The child that connects Heaven with Earth

needs to stay alive. If it dies,

the universe dies and has to be reborn again.

*C*hildren give the Earth another chance.

I have no idea who or what I am!

Nor do I care!

I wake up every morning to the miracle of day.

What more do I have to know?

The slow evolution of consciousness

from depression to joy,

from neurosis to inner peace and quiet,

from the mind's existential outhouse

to the heart's warmth

is about openness and acceptance of life

and all its responsibilities.

I once complained to Rudi
about how difficult my life was.

He pointed to a weed

growing in a crack in the New York City sidewalk.

"There's more life in that weed than in you," he said.

I never complained to him again.

"*O*ur growth

should never be at the expense of someone else."

Rudi

"*A*s we grow,

we can see that life exists

on many dimensions and at many levels.

We can see that we are superior in some ways

and less developed in others.

So, we can look at other people

and other situations and stay open,

understanding that we have the capacity

to take from everybody all there is to take, and

from everything all it has to offer."

Rudi

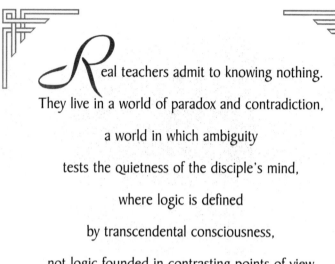

*R*eal teachers admit to knowing nothing.
They live in a world of paradox and contradiction,

a world in which ambiguity

tests the quietness of the disciple's mind,

where logic is defined

by transcendental consciousness,

not logic founded in contrasting points of view

vying for supremacy.

Ramana Maharshi asked the question: "Who am I?"

If we truly answer that question, if we peel all the

masks away, if we stop hiding behind the ego,

the answer is simple: "I am nothing."

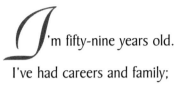I'm fifty-nine years old.

I've had careers and family;

I've made and lost money and made it again;

I've spent thirty years working on myself,

quieting my mind, opening my heart

and I've come to realize

I still haven't the foggiest idea

what I'm going to do when I grow up.

The child in me greets every day.

It doesn't want to destroy today

by worrying about tomorrow.

o one can take away from us

possessions we're not attached to;

no one can hurt us if we're not fearful.

We can only be hurt if we're protective of ourselves,

if we hide in the womb of our own anxiety,

if we set up psychological barriers

between ourselves and life.

'*I*'ve never seen an open-hearted person

who is not physically beautiful.

There's always a sparkle in their eye,

a childlike glow and innocence, love

and the richness of spirit coming through them.

Happy people are kind and loving people

who are drunk on life, who, in their own way,

are reminders of God's energy on Earth.

One has to choose a guru

the same way one chooses food in the supermarket:

Read the ingredients on the label

and listen to your inner voice.

*I*f teachings help you,

the results will manifest in day-to-day living.

It doesn't matter if the teaching is difficult.

Does it work? That's the important question.

If not, you spend your life clinging to fool's gold.

Time passes quickly and spiritual enlightenment's

delayed until the next lifetime

and the next lifetime and the next.

About the Author

Born in 1942, Stuart Perrin has trodden the spiritual path since he was sixteen. He studied literature, philosophy, acting, and poetry, and lived a Bohemian life in Europe and Africa until he was 25 and met his teacher, Albert Rudolph. Better known as Rudi, this iconoclastic spiritual teacher gave Eastern spirituality a new American slant, and Stuart Perrin has been carrying that slant forward ever since Rudi's death in 1973. His studies with Rudi gave Stuart a deep insight into how meditation and inner work can help a person find a way to live in the world and to be free of it at the same time. The author of four previous books, and an expert in Oriental art, Perrin ran a meditation center in Texas for nine years before moving to New York City, where he lived for 20 years. He subsequently moved to Woodstock, New York, and has since returned to New York City where he continues to teach spiritual work in the tradition of Rudi.

Hampton Roads Publishing Company

. . . for the evolving human spirit

Hampton Roads Publishing Company
publishes books on a variety of subjects including
metaphysics, health, visionary fiction,
and other related topics.

For a copy of our latest catalog,
call toll-free, 800-766-8009,
or send your name and address to:

Hampton Roads Publishing Company, Inc.
1125 Stoney Ridge Road
Charlottesville, VA 22902
e-mail: hrpc@hrpub.com
www.hrpub.com